Vitalis

The Prague Golem

THE PRAGUE GOLEM

Jewish Stories of the Ghetto

VITALIS

© Vitalis, 2002
  U Železné lávky 568/10
  CZ-118 00 Praha
  www.vitalis-verlag.com

Translation: Soňa Marešová
Typography: Cadis, Praha
Print: Finidr, Český Těšín

ISBN: 3-934774-46-6
ISBN: 80-7253-041-0

Contents

How the Jews Came to Bohemia 9

The Old-New Synagogue of Prague 14

Mordecai Maisel 19

The Quiet Jew 27

Rabbi Loew's Engagement 33

Rabbi Loew, the Benefactor of the Jews in Prague 35

The Wine Merchant and His Coachman 39

Beleles Street 43

The Creation of Golem 45

The Torah Scroll that Fell 47

Golem Is Enraged 49

Golem's End 52

Rabbi Loew and the Rose 54

Pinkas Street 57

How the Jews Came to Bohemia

According to old tradition [...] there should have been a flourishing town where the Jews had lived, on the area that is present-day Prague, already at the time of the Second Temple[1]. The town was, however, later destroyed and the inhabitants driven away. Princess Libuše who had founded Prague in 730 AD was generally known to be a prophetess. On her death-bed she called for her son Nezamysl and told him:

"I shall be at rest with my forefathers soon and before I go I want to reveal the future to you. At the time your grandson will reign over my people, a small foreign nation, rejected and oppressed, that worships only one God, will seek protection in our forests. May they be well received, may your grandson offer them protection for they will bring to the common land prosperity." When Hostivít[2] succeeded to the throne more than 100 years after the Princess had died, Libuše appeared to him in a dream and said: "The time has come for my prophecy to be fulfilled. A small, tormented nation that worships only one God shall come to your throne looking for help. May you receive them affably, hospitably and mercifully, and may you offer them protection and shelter."

After the Wends[3] wreaked havoc upon the Lithuanians and Muscovites, drove the inhabitants away, conquered the land and choose it as their seat, a Jewish community was driven from the Muscovite area. Those miserable, unfortunate people roamed the world without shelter for ten years; eventually they reached Bohemia exhausted from their wandering. They asked for a hearing at the ruler, the Prince Hostivít. Their request was granted. They were told to send two of their elders to the Prince. The Prince received them

---

[1] An era of the Jewish history (circa 300 BC – 100 AD) which ended with the destruction of the Second Temple of Jerusalem in 70 AD
[2] Hostivít (died about 870 AD): legendary Bohemian Prince
[3] Wends: earlier general term for the Slavs

cordially and asked: "Who are you and what is your wish?" The delegates replied: "We are a small nation and we call ourselves after the progenitor of our nation – Israel. We lived peacefully in one of the provinces in the Muscovite area until a powerful enemy came, conquered the land and drove its inhabitants away. We have wandered restlessly through the far wide world, the moorland was our bed, a stone was our pillow, the heavens our roof. We are a peace-loving nation, small in number and weak in strength. We follow the teaching of Moses; we worship one God who is Almighty, all knowing, all righteous and all embracing, whose glory fills the whole globe. We humbly beseech you, Oh Prince, that you might find it favourable to let us build our dwellings here. Give us your mighty protection, Oh Prince, that we

View of the Old-New Synagogue and the Jewish Town Hall in Prague

may be your loyal subjects and beseech our God to grant glory and victory to you and your people." Immediately the Prince recognised that this was the nation whose arrival had been prophesied. But he said wisely: "Await the answer in two days. Come to see me the day after tomorrow and I shall tell you if I can grant your request."

On the morning of the next day he assembled all the country gentlemen[4] and said: "My predecessor Libuše prophesied before she died that a nation seeking for help would come to our land. When I succeeded to the throne, Libuše appeared in my dream to tell me that the time would come soon for her prophecy to be fulfilled. She also told me that I should support those oppressed people who worship only one God and should give them protection. And look, two elderly members of such a community approached me yesterday. They belong to the ancient and venerable Jewish nation. They have asked for permission to settle in our forests and there is no doubt that these are the people described by my ancestor. I would like to give them a place to settle in our country because they will bring us good fortune and their blessing. Anyway I shall send for them tomorrow because I would like to hear your views first."

"Do as said!" the assembly replied. "Libuše said, these people will bring us prosperity and give us their blessing."

The Prince gave the Jews an order permitting them to settle on the left bank of the River Vltava in the environs of present-days Újezd[5]. The Jews kept their word given to the Prince. The oldest Bohemian chronicler, called Cosmas, already describes how the Jews of Prague had given Prince Hostivít, when at war with the Germans, great support supplying both provisions and finances so that the Prince succeeded in expelling the Germans from Bohemia.

So the Jews lived in Bohemia already in the times of paganism long before the Christian faith had become familiar there.

Under the reign of Bořivoj[6] who allowed himself to be baptised in 900 AD the Jewish population increased so much that the area they inhabited became too small for them. They asked the Prince for more space and were granted a site on the right bank of the River Vltava which is now Josefské město, previously known as the Jewish Town. A large area was donated to the Jewish community and the people who had no or little money had the approval of the Prince to build their houses there. Also a large piece of ground near

---

[4] country gentlemen: lower Bohemian aristocracy
[5] Újezd: an old settlement-area in Prague where Karmelitská Street is today
[6] Bořivoj I (died before 890 AD): the first baptised Bohemian Prince, the information concerning the year 900 AD does not coincide with historical facts

the Jewish Town was given them for a cemetery. Building of the Jewish Town began in 907 AD. Initially, it consisted of thirty, mostly wooden, houses only. Higher architecture was not wide-spread in Bohemia at that time and for larger constructions master-builders from distant Italy would have had to be called in. Naturally this was possible only for the Prince and for some of the elite and nobles, such as the country gentlemen. The first synagogue of the Prague Jewish community was therefore built of wood.

Since the Prague Jews came from the Muscovite area, they were attired in "Russian" dress and they had established the Polish rites in their synagogue, still used in the Old-New Synagogue and partly in other smaller synagogues. The first Rabbi[7] of the Prague Jewish community was Malchi, a great scholar, who was born in Cracow. The Jewish population continued to grow and remained under the protection of the rights granted them by the Prince. These rights were even extended on several occasions when the Jews excelled exceptionally. Such as in 1150 during the reign of King Vladislav[8] when the sectarians emerged. They called themselves flagellants and began to defame the ruling religion, and the whole nation was tempted to convert. The King ordered that all flagellants must leave Prague and the country. Being too weak to oppose the King's will the flagellants then chose the Jews as victims of their revenge. During the night the Jewish Town was attacked but the aggressors had been betrayed. The Jewish butchers, who were a large group at that time, gathered at the first warning signal. Each holding a butcher's knife in one hand, and a burning torch in the other, they rushed towards the furious crowd. Which, although predominant, was panic stricken and fled. However, the Jewish butchers chased them and drew them away from the town.

King Vladislav had the Jewish butchers called to be praised for their brave and courageous behaviour. And he stressed how glad he was that they had protected the Jewish Town against the attack and that they had chased the invaders away from the town. From then on, the Jewish butchers were allowed to bear the Czech double-tailed lion in their coat of arms as a reward. All subsequent Bohemian kings confirmed this privilege. King Vladislav also gave the Prague Jews the right to fortify the Jewish Town and to surround it with gates that were to be closed at night to prevent similar attacks.

From the time of Vladislav to that of George of Poděbrady[9] the Jews lived in undisturbed peace despite the strong upheavals that affected Bohemia. From

---

[7] Rabbi: 'My Master' the title of a wise man in the Mishnah period, a name for the Torah scholar or the Chasid leader

[8] Vladislav II (born circa 1110, died 1174): Bohemian Prince and King

[9] George of Poděbrady [in Czech: Jiří z Poděbrad] (born 1420, died 1471): an important Bohemian King

then on, defamations against the Jews arose from time to time. On several occasions the Jews were expelled from the country only to be called back soon after it was proved that these defamations were hatred of the lowest order. But the Jews fulfilled their duties loyally and were always quiet and unselfish Bohemian citizens. The God who does not abandon the people of Israel,......let them again find mercy before the monarchs of the land.

Interior of the Old-New Synagogue

The Old-New Synagogue of Prague

With the exception of the synagogue at Worms where a Jewish community was living at the time of the Second Temple, the Old-New Synagogue is the oldest preserved Jewish synagogue. The intact west wall of the Temple of Jerusalem that has survived the ravages of time can be considered no more than a ruin.

The Old-New Synagogue, preserved in Gothic-Germanic style, is typical of medieval architecture in Europe, of which the most perfect examples are to be found in Germany. Three parts of the Synagogue can be distinguished from the outside: the men's section, the women's section and a small chapel where the divine services are mostly held for those who are not allowed to visit the synagogue at the time of common divine service. The two latter parts, however, the women's section in particular seem to be of a later date. The entrance is located on the southern side with short flight of steps leading downwards into the building.

The Prague Jewish community had grown so much that in the first wooden synagogue there was not enough room for believers. In the year 4690 after the creation of the world, which is 929 in the common calendar of the Christian era, prominent members of the Prague Jewish community met and decided that a large stone synagogue will be built. A desolate hill full of stones, undergrowth and mostly rotten trees in the Jewish Town should be levelled and a new synagogue built there. When digging over the hill the workers discovered some completely intact walls made from white stone blocks. They seemed to be walls of an old house of God. The supposition changed into certainty when they found a Torah scroll on a deerskin and a few prayer books written in Hebrew.

At that time there were two delegates of the Jerusalem community in Prague who were to collect money to support the poor of the Holy City. They were men of great wisdom, with profound knowledge of the Talmud and Rabbi Chisdai who was a great Talmud scholar in the Jewish community in Prague asked them for advice.

They were in doubt especially regarding the walls. The two men from Jerusalem said: "The Jews must have lived here already at the time of the Second Temple and they must have built this house of God. These stones have been consecrated once, and they are well preserved and are usable. They should be used for the new building. We advise you also to build this synagogue like the one in Tiberias, which was built according to the Holy Temple of Jerusalem. May you therefore build "schkufim atumim" windows, which means that the window openings should be wide at the outer wall and become narrower through the whole thickness of the wall to the inside. Two pillars should carry a mighty vault and a few steps should lead down into the synagogue. The synagogue should be situated below the level of the surrounding landscape because it is

said: "We call you from the depths, Oh Lord!" If you build the synagogue in this way, the Almighty shall listen to you at this place and He shall protect this house of prayer mercifully against destruction by fire and water."

Not all members of the Jewish community were satisfied with this advice. Some thought it would be a violation of the memory of the Jerusalem Temple. However when the prophet Elijah appeared in a dream to Sch'lomo Kun's, who was the head of the Jewish community, and told him to follow the advice of those men, everybody agreed. The two Palestinians left Prague loaded with rich donations for the poor of the Holy City. A Saxon architect, by the name of Lirensky, was engaged to carry out construction of the synagogue. Building work proceeded quickly, and the new synagogue was consecrated two years later, at the Shavuoth[10] holiday

---

[10] Shavuoth: a two-day holiday; one of three Pilgrim festivals of a Hebrew year; the giving of the Law to Moses on Mount Sinai is commemorated during this feast. Shavuoth is identical with the Christian Whitsun feast.

Studying the Talmud

Life in the ghetto

in 931 AD. The synagogue was called the Old-New Synagogue because the new synagogue was built from the stones of the old one.

No substantial changes were made to the inside of the building ever since it was built. But over the thousand years its walls became the deepest black colour. The name of God was written in verse on them and for that reason they could not be painted white. But for the Jews, this thousand-year-old dust represents their sacred past because the blood of their fathers is now stuck to the walls. It was in the year 1388 under the reign of Wenceslas the Lazy[11] when an unrestrained crowd attacked the Jewish Town. The Jews should renounce their faith or die. The Jews were surprised and too weak to resist the numerically superior mob. Old men, young men, women and children fled to the Old-New Synagogue. The furious crowd followed them and the door was broken open by force. Nobody wanted to renounce their faith and so they were all – children in front of their mothers, fathers in front of their sons – brutally massacred. The blood of the martyrs splashed up onto the walls of the house of God.

King Wenceslas let the atrocity go unpunished and even without legal investigation. The case gave rise to great discontent among the country's seniors and among most of the people as well. The never ending excesses and outrageous cruelties of the King who had had the Queen ripped to pieces by his hunting dogs, his confessor thrown into the River Vltava and many other respectable men of the land executed, aroused the people's wrath.

It is remarkable that the dignified building of the Old-New Synagogue survived intact the many fires that had raged in the Jewish Town. During the fire in 1558 two white doves were seen on top of the synagogue that flew up and disappeared into the clouds after the fire had been extinguished completely – when the Old-New Synagogue no longer needed special protection.

More than sixty curtains for the Holy Ark[12], richly decorated with gold and pearls, are kept in the synagogue. One of them is a donation by Karpel Sachs, the first Parneß[13] of the Prague Jewish community, from 1601. Another one is from the legendary Jekew Schmiles and his wife who ran their own mint in the Jewish Town on the square that was then called Dreibrunnenplatz.

---

[11] Wenceslas IV [in Czech: Václav] (died 1419): Bohemian king, Roman-German Emperor; the son of the legendary Charles IV

[12] Holy Ark; a case in the synagogue which serves for keeping the Torah scrolls; it is an instrument of holy worship

[13] Parneß: the chief representative of the Jewish community

The coverage of the Prague Haggadah (a woodcut from 1526)

Mordecai Maisel

The surname Maisel deserves to be one of the most famous names among the Jews in Prague because there was no other person so charitable and modest, and never had any Jew done so much for his fellow-believers. It was he who had the muddy streets of the Jewish Town paved, and he also had the beautiful Jewish Town Hall built. Two synagogues, the Maisel-Synagogue and the High Synagogue are also reminders of his charity. The bath-house for women was also built through his generosity, as well as the poorhouse and the orphanage. The origin of such immeasurable wealth is revealed in the following legend.

Some two hundred years ago, the Primas[14] by the name of Jizchak was on his way back to Prague after a long journey. In the twilight the coachman lost his way in a dense forest. He drove on, once to the right, then to the left, over sticks and stones. Suddenly the horses shied, began to snort and rear up on their hind legs, scaring the coachman and the Mayor travelling in the coach. As the two of them looked around for the cause, they caught sight of a small bluish light in the distance. Something flickered through the trees and gradually grew into flaming mountain illuminating the entire surroundings. Rabbi Jizchak, a fearless and hearty man, had the eyes of the horses blindfolded and went towards the place from where the flames were raging. As he approached, he saw two small dwarfs with long greybeards busily filling their sacks with gold and silver pieces from the glowing heap, without uttering a word or noticing the newcomers. For a while Rabbi Jizchak silently watched them at work and then asked them: "Who are you filling the sacks for?" "Not for you", one of them answered angrily, then he and the gold and the sacks vanished. Only a few pieces glittered scattered on the ground. The other dwarf was more friendly and said: "It is for someone from your nation but with your question you have done harm to the treasure." Then he revealed that the treasure would be transferred after the wedding of his daughter. He also agreed that the Rabbi might exchange his money for the few golden pieces that were scattered on the ground. The Mayor took from his purse three pieces of gold, threw them on the ground, and picked up three pieces from the ground in exchange. At that moment everything vanished and there he stood, alone in the darkness. The Mayor returned to the coach, reassured the coachman that the appearances

---

[14] Primas (in Latin: primus 'the first'): the Mayor

were no more than burning piles of wood. Since the horses had calmed down again, they could now drive away. Before long the forest became thinner and thinner and the Mayor arrived in Prague by the dawn of a new day.

The curious Mayor could not make out who was supposed to be the unknown owner of such treasure. He thought it must be divine providence from God. He wrapped each of those pieces of gold in scraps of paper and threw one of them out of the window onto the street. Despite the fact that the house was in broad, busy street, the gold piece lay there unnoticed until the evening. Rabbi Jizchak had intended to have it brought up, when a cheerful, barefoot and poorly dressed boy appeared on the street. He hesitated in front of the rabbi's house, looked around anxiously and in a flash picked up the piece of gold and ran off. The Mayor shook his head thoughtfully and said: "What a fine millionaire!"

Displeased with the whimsical hand of fate he could hardly wait for the following day to test his destiny once more. But the same boy again picked up the second piece of gold.

"It is strange," said the scholarly Mayor to himself. "Such an uncared-for boy! What does he have in common with this? The Lord moves in mysterious ways, anyway!" On the third day the last piece of gold was thrown onto the street and indeed, the boy collected that one too! The wise Rabbi Jizchak hesitated no longer that this discrepid-looking boy would one day get the great treasure from the forest. He wanted to know whether he really deserved so much wealth of the Lord. He had the town crier called and ordered him to announce the loss of the golden pieces with the request that the finder might reimburse them to the owner according to the Law of Moses. In this way the Mayor wanted to discover both the character and the origin of the boy.

Shortly afterwards the boy appeared at house of the Mayor. He told him that he had come by the three pieces of gold in a most wondrous way. The night before he had had a dream indicating that he would make a discovery. Now he would like to return it to the owner according to the Law of Moses. But he has only two pieces of gold since he had given one piece to his mother for her shop. However, she would return it as soon as possible. Then the Mayor asked him with a smile: "You could have kept all three, who would have betrayed you when no-one has seen you? What a fool you are!"

For a moment the boy looked at him in astonishment, then said with devout ardour: "May the God of Israel prevent me from doing so. I would rather be poor and honest than make a fortune in an illegal way. Here are your pieces of gold."

With his heart filled with emotions, the venerable Mayor approached the boy, put both hands on the boy's head and said with solemn voice: "May God bless you and be merciful unto you! You deserve to be a beloved child of our God. – Tell me, my son, would you like to stay with me? You will be happy in my house."

"Your Honour, I cannot do so," replied the boy. "I have an old blind father whom I have to care for when my mother is at work in her shop. Who would accompany him to the place of worship three times a day to say his prayers? No, I cannot stay in your house even if you gave me your whole fortune. A stranger can never replace the devotion of a child. Above everything I prize the commandment: Honour your father and your mother, so that you may live long."

The Mayor asked the boy kindly the name and profession of his father. When his found that it was Schalum Maisel and that he had worked as a carrier before he went blind, he gave both pieces of gold back to the boy and sent him home.

A few days later, the Maisel family was sitting at table and they discussed this event over and over again. The father praised the noble-mindedness of the Mayor in fact. He thought that the rich do sometimes have such moods and that they soon disappear like dreams. A man should not rely on the charity of the sons of the earth, as King David once said. And Mordecai, already fifteen years old could soon attach a rope to his shoulders with which to carry loads and become a carrier like he him-

A tombstone in the Old Jewish Cemetery

21

self and his father before him. He should be pious and righteous and then he will never lack God's blessing.

Then the door opened and the Rabbi Jizchak entered. After greeting each other, he sat down humbly and said that he had some things to discuss with the parents and that meanwhile the boy could play outside with his friends. Then he asked father Maisel whether he would let Mordecai visit him because he would like to bring him up as his own son and he would enable him to study. The embarrassed father objected that there should be no trade with children, and that Mordecai was the only child left from his eight children. Rabbi Jizchak said quickly: "Let me only finish what I have to say. You could keep your son with you, he would eat and drink at your home, but please let him come to my place for few hours every day so that he would learn something and would become a person of importance. Because your son should not become a carrier," he stressed emphatically.

"I want him to become a competent and clever merchant. I am pleased with him and would like to give him the hand of my daughter Sulamit in marriage, if he stays this way."

The two old people fell silent because they were not prepared for such an offer. Surely, had they known what the Mayor knew, that such a treasure was to be given to their son from the Almighty, they would most certainly have had even more objections. Filled with emotion the father could only say: "It is decided by God that this plentiful blessing from heaven will come to him through your hands."

"We are therefore united," said Rabbi Jizchak and he rose from his seat. "As for now it should remain only between ourselves. Neither your son nor my daughter should know of this matter until the right time comes. God be with you!" The Mayor went on his way and left the astonished parents alone with their pleasure.

Five years went by very quickly and pleasantly for young Maisel. During that time, his body had gained in strength and beauty and his mind had developed so much that he was considered the kindest most charming scholarly boy. His good heart remained unchanged in his love and helpfulness towards his poor parents. He was still taking his father three times a day to the synagogue and helping his mother in the small ironmonger's shop. Sulamit grew up and became even more beautiful and Rabbi Jizchak noticed with paternal pride the growing affection between the two young people. When the young Maisel was twenty years old and Sulamit turned sixteen, they got engaged.

The Jewish community in Prague was confused with this extraordinary connection between the wealthy Mayor and the poor carrier. However, the Mayor let the people talk because he knew what he knew and after a year time the loving pair was married in the yard of the Old-New Synagogue.

When all seven wedding days passed, Rabbi Jizchak thought it high time to pick up the promised sacks of gold for his son-in-law. He had his carriage harnessed and with Maisel they set out for a trip. They arrived at the forest in the evening, again at the place where the Mayor had had that miraculous experience six years before. They stayed there nearly all night and neither the glowing mountain, nor the dwarfs, nor neither the sacks of gold, nor the piles of gold appeared.

The disgruntled Mayor eventually turned back and was consoled only by his thoughts that it was not the right time yet.

Weeks, months even a year elapsed; Rabbi Jizchak made several more trips to the mysterious place but in vain. The sacks of gold did not appear.

Finally, his belief in the miracle began to diminish and the Rabbi thought it must have been a spook of an evil spirit who wanted to lead him towards such a connection so harmful for his dignity. Because of his disappointment, he became more sullen and bitter day by day and he treated his son-in-law with cold contempt.

The young Maisel, who had no idea of the expectations of his father-in-law, was so hurt by this unloving behaviour that he decided to set up his own household and not to eat the bread of charity and not to live on sufferance of his father-in-law any longer. For as Sulamit agreed to this, the young pair left the paternal home and rented a dwelling for themselves. Maisel took over the small store with scrap-iron and through his diligence he was able to turn it into an important store. Without the support of his father-in-law, he bought himself a house and also one for his parents and even saved up a little money. And so he lived, pleased with what the God of his fathers had given him.

As the time passed, Maisel's house became a sanctuary for the needy and the oppressed. One day, when the generous Maisel was in his store, a peasant dressed in smock came to the vault to buy some pieces of iron as he said.

After he had chosen what he wanted and put it together, he said: "Mister, I have no money now but I need the things urgently. Would you be so kind as to wait some time and I will pay you then honestly, I will."

"If you need the things so urgently, I will give them to you without money. I don't know you but you will not deceive me. Go in the name of God and come again whenever you need something," said Maisel to him.

The visibly happy and pleased peasant then offered him a promising business deal. He said that for many years he had a large iron box at home and that nobody was able to open it. He himself would never have any use for this iron box and he would sell it to the merchant after having it weighed. After the promise that he would get two kreutzers for every pound of usable iron, the peasant went away with his pieces of iron.

Three days later, he arrived with a huge box in a coach in front of the Maisel's iron-store. The box was unloaded with great effort and put onto scales. The sum was calculated and the peasant was delighted that after having paid all his debts, he even had a few florins left over for him.

The following night, Maisel was about to try to open the box with a hammer and chisel. However, when tapped it the first time, it jumped open by itself. The astonished merchant saw that it was filled only with rolls of paper. He quickly unwrapped one of them and saw that pieces of gold were blinking at him. Silently, he took one roll after another and he hid it in a secret place without telling anyone, not even his wife. He knew the weakness of the women who are unable to hold their tongues, even at graveside.

Now Maisel was one of the richest Jews in the community but he was careful not to let it leak out to the public. The man might come back, Maisel thought, and his conscience refused to profit from a treasure that had come to him only through the innocence and ignorance of a peasant.

He had been waiting for more than one year for the return of the peasant about whom he knew absolutely nothing. But then he thought he must be entitled to use the treasure given to him from God.

He went to the Chief Rabbi and he said: "Sir! The God of Israel blessed the work of my hands and I have decided to build a house where His name shall be praised. Gold is here, invite the best master-builders to erect the most beautiful synagogue in Prague. But you are not allowed to call it by my name."

The devout Rabbi was surprised at the man's humility; he gave him his blessing and promised to do everything as he wished.

Finally, the masterpiece was finished, people came from near and far to visit the new magnificent temple and everybody praised the unknown benefactor who had financed it.

One feast day, the synagogue was consecrated. The elite of the town was present there and the Rabbi gave a heart-rending speech that ended with: "Praise be Israel! For you have such a good man in your midst! Step forward, you humble soul! Why are you hiding among the crowd when you are really one of the greatest?" As he was talking, he pointed towards the corner where Maisel was hiding with embarrassment. "Step out of the darkness, you light of the Lord!" the Rabbi called excitedly. "You, Mordecai Maisel, I am calling you!"

When the people heard his name, a solemn silence spread through the crowd. It gradually changed into a gentle murmur and ended in loud jubilant rejoicing. Countless hands raised the modest benefactor on high to bring him forward to the steps where the Chief Rabbi was standing. Full of humility, Maisel lowered his eyes, the Chief Rabbi placed his hands on his head to bless him quietly. Then he rose again and solemnly pronounced the blessing which ended with the plea: "May the foundations of this house remain undisturbed until once through your paternal benevolence your children will assemble again in the Temple of Jerusalem. Amen."

Rabbi Jizchak who as Mayor occupied the seat nearest the Torah shrine was beside himself with joy. As soon as the Chief Rabbi had finished and descended the steps, the rapturous father-in-law went up to his son-in-law and without a word pressed him hard on his chest. Everybody was pushing through the crowd to express their pleasure and their sincere good wishes, to the delighted Mayor and his son-in-law. The people streamed happily from the temple to the house of the Chief Rabbi where a huge banquet was held for everyone without exception.

Mordecai Maisel remained a rich man for the rest of his life but he did not deviate from his piety and humility. He never accepted any function or title. His modesty is still praised among the Jews in Prague when they say: "Maisel had no place reserved in the synagogue."

As an unknown donor he had to buy himself a place in the synagogue which he had financed. How much good he had done, we have just told. Even today you can read about his good deeds in the Maisel-Synagogue, namely in worn Hebrew verses engraved into the marble. His whole life was a chain of continuous good deeds.

Yet it is also said that the last hour of his life was not his best hour. On his death-bed, Mordecai Maisel told his wife to immediately give a large sum of money for the poor of the ghetto[15] to Rabbi Loew. Angrily, his wife refused to do so and thus embittered his last hour. After his death Mordecai Maisel's wealth vanished into oblivion. As Maisel had no children, the authorities declared his property invalid and ordered a confiscation of the entire legacy for their own purposes. There was a lot of bad blood during the court proceedings but Mordecai Maisel could know nothing of this any more.

---

[15] ghetto: enclosed separate district in Venice where the Jewish population was isolated from the rest of the population from 1516; also districts where the Jews lived in other towns were called ghettos later on

View of the Old Town in Prague and the ghetto (1769)

The Quiet Jew

A tailor whose name was Reb Schime Scheftels had lived in one of the poor houses in the upper part of the Jewish Town in Prague more than six hundred years ago. He was hardly able to provide for his wife and his three children miserably and even his grandmother the very old "Schammeste" Ziperl had to help him a lot so that he and his family would not die of hunger. Also she worked in the women's section of the Old-New Synagogue where she gave "assistance" especially to women who either had no experience with the rituals or were not literate. Schime Scheftels was not much respected because of his trade, neither did he enjoy much respectability from the Prague Jewish community. He was not a learned man and could only read "Blatt Gemara"[16] with difficulty. Everything concerning daily life, apart from things connected with his trade, was of no interest to him. He only loved his wife and children with a deep and quiet tenderness. Because of his calm nature he was soon nicknamed "the quiet Jew". His shy and simple ways made him the target for ridicule which he let pass without a word. His grandmother, however, could not ignore this happening to her grandson and shouted to the mockers repeatedly: "Leave my Schimele alone and remember – still waters run deep!" And she was right.

It was a morning in June in 1286 of the common calendar. There was a hectic atmosphere in Prague's Jewish Town since it was the day before the Shavuoth holiday. Široká Street of the Prague ghetto was like a flower garden. Women were everywhere offering flowers, only flowers, at street stalls along the way from the Old-New Synagogue up to the Golden Lane, for people to decorate their houses ready for the Shavuoth days. Incredibly chaotic

---

[16] Gemara: besides Mishnah the most important part of the Talmud

crowds were pushing and shoving in the shops and narrow streets when doing the last shopping for the holiday. Suddenly this noisy life changed into a curious silence. A huge stocky man with a tall staff adorned with a large knob in his right hand and accompanied by a gang of children came from Rabbi Street. It was Reb Leser, the town-crier of the Prague Jewish community. He stopped in the middle of Široká Street and hit the ground three times with his staff. There was a breathless silence for everyone knew that an important event was about to be heard. As soon as Reb Leser finished his announcement which he had begun with "Hört, liebe reboßaj"[17], it was quickly spread from mouth to mouth: "The King is coming!" Early in the morning a courier from the Prague Castle arrived in the Jewish Town and announced in the Jewish Town Hall that King Wenceslas II with his wife Judith would be coming to the Jewish Town to visit the sights.

After that Rob Leser had made known this news in all streets of the ghetto a real commotion broke out. The whole Jewish Town wanted to greet the King. Everything was hastily being prepared so as to give him the most festive of welcome. The Minha prayer[19] was held in the synagogues already at noon in celebration of the visit, the representatives of the community gathered in front of the Town Hall quite two hours before the arrival of the King. In their midst was the Roschhakohol Reb Feiwel in official attire with mortarboard and his buckle shoes and Rabbi Jonathan, the Chief Rabbi of the Bohemian Jews, dressed in silk coat and a tall fur-trimmed cap. The streets where the King was going to walk were full of people. The entire Prague ghetto was aglow with excitement.

When the bells of the Church of Our Lady of Týn announced the King's arrival at the gate of the Old-New Synagogue, jubilant cries filled the air, following the Royal couple wherever they appeared. In the Town Hall Square, their Majesties received homage from the representatives of the community. Then they visited the Old-New Synagogue and, celebrated by the crowd, they set out on their return journey. Suddenly, the enthousiastic applause turned into a horrifying scream. From one of the houses in Beleles Street a brick fell right in front of the King. Though uninjured, King Wenceslas left the place at once in a terrible rage. The Jewish community was seized by anxiety and fear because

---

[17] courteous form of address (reboßaj is plural form of rabbi) with this approximate meaning: "My dear Lord Teacher, listen!"

[18] Wenceslas II. [in Czech: Václav] (born 1271, died 1305): Bohemian King from 1278, the son of King Přemysl Otakar II

[19] an evening prayer

they knew that this would have horrific consequences for all of them.

When the whole community gathered in the Old-New Synagogue for divine worship in the evening, Beth-din-Schammes[20], the servant of the Rabbinical college, brought the Chief Rabbi a letter with Royal Seal. King Wenceslas ordered the Rabbi to notify the community that if the evil offender who had thrown the brick were not delivered to the authorities within eight days, then the whole Jewish Town would be plundered and its inhabitants driven away on the ninth day. The entire community was terrified. All efforts to find the guilty man immediately after the attack were unsuccessful. Nobody was found in the house from which the brick had fallen. Everyone was on the streets among the spectators at that time. It was suggested to the Royal authorities that the mishap might have been caused through carelessness during the reconstruction of the house, especially on the cornice. But the explanation was rejected. On the second day of Shavuoth holiday the Rosh hakohol[21] asked for an audience with the State Chancellor of the King whose name was Zawish of Rosenberg but this was refused. He was told scornfully that there were only five days left and the murderer must be at the Royal Castle.

The Jews of Prague were in deep

Student of the Talmud

---

[20] Schammes: a synagogal servant
[21] 'the head of the community'

despair and they saw the end of their days. Rabbi Jonathan ordered three fasting and expiatory days for the community after the Shavuoth days were over. They passed and still no solution was found. The iron gates of the ghetto were now closed even during the day because the Jews were afraid of the fury of the mob. On such occasions, the mob is ready to demonstrate its patriotic loyalty through hatred of the Jews. No Jew dared to leave the Jewish Town. Prayers of lamentation were said at the Old Jewish cemetery and in the synagogues, women lamented over the graves, clutching their children tight. Old Schammeste Ziperl was sitting in front of the Old-New Synagogue in deep misery, mumbling to herself: "The fathers ate sour grapes and children's teeth will be harsh."

On the 13th Sivan[22], after the last and eighth day when the time limit for the Prague Jewish community had elapsed, a huge crowd of people waited in front of the gates of the Prague Jewish ghetto. Armed with axes, maces and other weapons they were ready to start plundering immediately the gate opened. All men, women and children, the entire community gathered in the Old-New Synagogue. Only one person was missing – Reb Schime Scheftels, the "quiet Jew". He kissed his wife and his children as he always did, he left and did not come back. The community would surely not have noticed he was missing, had not his grief-stricken grandmother Ziperl been crying: "My poor quiet Schimele, what has happened to you?"

Weak murmurs of interest arose in the Jewish community threatened by the imminent disaster, when news about the disappearance of the "quiet Jew" was brought in. Moreover, it was spread incredibly quickly after Rabbi Jonathan stepped onto the elevated Almemar[23] and ordered silence with a sweep of his hand. "The community is saved from the imminent disaster," he declared, "but, at what a price. One of us has, with few words, as he has always done, sacrificed himself for the sake of Israel. Last night Reb Schime Scheftels, the "quiet Jew", went to the King's castle unbeknown to anyone and presented himself as the man who had tried to assassinate the King. We all know, however, that he is innocent and his memory shall stay sacred, as a sacrifice, in God's name. His sacrifice shall be accepted soon, the King has decided that Schime Scheftel will die."

The happiness over the miraculous rescue turned into painful mourning. The heroism of the "quiet Jew" was an inexplicable and mysterious miracle for the hearts of many people. But only one heart broke after the announcement. When old Schammeste Ziperl who was sitting in the women's section of the synagogue heard that her grandson had saved the Prague Jewish community,

---

[22] Sivan: the ninth month in the Jewish calendar, it corresponds with May – June approximately

[23] Almemar, Almemor: a platform for the reading of the Torah

she screamed for joy: "My quiet dear Schimele!" and fell over, dead.

The gates of the town were opened. Armed riders withheld the mob that had wanted to invade and plunder the community. Their leader read out the King's Edict saying that the wrongdoer was now in hands of the King and the Jewish Town was free of the impending punishment. Furthermore, the culprit would be thrown down from the very house where he had committed his crime. Through the Old School's gate mounted mercenaries were riding. In the middle was Reb Schime in chains, accompanied by Rabbi Jonathan. They stopped at the house in the Beleles Street where eight days ago the incident had happened. The whole Jewish Town was gathered there. Not a single eye was dry when the humble tailor who had sacrificed himself for the sake of the entire community passed by without even looking up. He greeted his wife and his children and was led up onto the roof of the house that was his place of execution. The mounted soldiers were standing in front of the house with their pikes pointing upwards.

Reb Schime turned once more to the east and then jumped onto the pikes shouting: "Sch'ma Jisraeel, adonoj elohenu, adonoj echod[24]."

For three long days the entire Prague Jewish community mourned over their martyr, the light of soul had burned for him in the Old-New Synagogue for ten days. On the third day after the death of the "quiet Jew" Rabbi Jonathan had a dream saying that Schime was a descendant of the prophet Zechariah who was killed by Israel because he protested against the decadent customs.

Zawish of Rosenberg, State Chancellor of King Wenceslas II, died on the scaffold guilty of high treason two years after Reb Schimes had died a martyr's death. Fifteen minutes before his death he had Rabbi Jonathan from the Prague ghetto called and confessed that two years ago he had instigated one of his servants to throw a brick at the King in a street of the Jewish ghetto. He knew this crime would be ascribed to the Jews. The Rabbi had to promise him that he would take care of the family of the "quiet Jew."

---

[24] the opening words of the Jewish confession of faith which proclaims the unity of God

Old meat shops in the Jewish Town in Prague

Rabbi Loew's Engagement

In 1513 a son was born to the highly esteemed Rabbi Bezalel ben Chajim, a descendant of the Raw Hai Gaon, an offspring of the King David in the male line. The father who was well known for his piety in the old town of Worms upon Rhine named the child Jehuda Loew after a verse in the Bible. The child came into this world to protect the Jews against malicious defamation and suspicions originating from the Christians.

Some years passed. There were probably enough ample opportunities to perfect oneself in the rabbinical teachings in Worms. However, it was a practice of the Jewish boys to keep faithfully the word given to their fathers to travel to far distant climes and to quench the thirst for knowledge in the footsteps of the legendary teachers and masters. Jehuda, the boy, had hardly grown when he moved to Prague.

The rich and devout man called Reb Samuel Schmelke Reich, known as Rich Schmelke, lived in Prague at that time. And when his virtuous daughter Pearl wanted to get engaged, Loew was chosen to be her future husband. So he became engaged to Pearl at the age of fifteen according to the custom of that time. In order to fulfil the wish of Reb Schmelke, the young Loew soon moved to Poland to study at the famous School of Rabbi Sch'lomo Lurje in Lublin. He was at that time the head of the Jewish Diaspora and he shone as the biggest star in the heaven of Jewish science.

Very soon after that Mr. Schmelke lost his fortune in an unsuccessful undertaking and so he was unable to provide the promised dowry and carry out the arrangements of the marriage. So he wrote to Loew who had already reached the age of eighteen, that he was not able to provide the dowry for his daughter. Therefore Loew does not have to feel bound to his vow; he will be forgiven and allowed to marry another woman.

Loew replied to it: "I trust in God's help and I shall wait until He helps you to raise the funds for the dowry and for the wedding arrangements. Furthermore

I will consider the engagement broken, only when and not until then that your daughter would be married.

As the financial situation of Reb Schmelke was not improving, Pearl opened a store with salt and bread and other groceries to help her parents.

Almost a decade passed. Loew remained engaged, he was not married but he devoted himself to studies of the science. Therefore he was called "Loew the Bochur".[25]

One day troops of soldiers happened to be in the streets of Prague. There was a high-ranking officer riding with them. When he was passing Pearl's store, he stuck his sword into the large loaf of bread that was used for display in the shop. Pearl was frightened and cried out. But she recovered immediately and asked the officer not to take her bread without paying for it because she has to feed her old parents from the meagre income from the store.

The officer took the saddle from his horse and threw it inside the shop saying: "I am hungry but I have no money to pay for the loaf of bread, so take this saddle instead." Therewith he rode away.

Pearl was astonished when she took the saddle to find inside it a pile of golden ducats! She hurried home, and with tears of joy told her parents about the treasure she had been given in such a miraculous way.

Reb Schmelke realized then that the officer could have been none else than the prophet Elijah and that this new stroke of luck is owed to the merits of his son-in-law. Immediately he wrote to Loew that the heavens had sent him help in wonderful way and he asked him to come to Prague as soon as possible to celebrate his wedding.

Loew came to Prague, married his pious Pearl and it was not long before he was called to be a Rabbi in Posen.

---

[25] Bocher, also bochur, bachur: a student of the Talmud, unmarried man

Rabbi Loew, the Benefactor of the Jews in Prague

Rabbi Jehuda Loew ben Bezalel had worked in Posen for a longer period before he was called by the Emperor Rudolph II[26] to come to Prague Castle. There he was appointed to be the Chief Rabbi of the Jewish Town and he held this office until he died.

Rabbi Loew lived in Široká Street in the Jewish Town. Above the door of his house he had a lion with a grape engraved into a stone to indicate his descent.

At that time, numerous Jewish immigrants from Russia and the Balkans settled in Prague and the town became a place of refuge for people from Spain and Portugal who were seeking asylum from the inquisition. In addition ordinary colonists from German towns and the famous Talmudic scholars also came.

At the time when Rabbi Loew had settled down in Prague, new heavy blows threatened the fate of the Jews in Prague – they were supposed to be expelled from the country. Rabbi Loew wanted to protect his people from this and he made intercessions to the Emperor. As the valet rejected him, he looked for another way.

Rabbi Loew was waiting in the crowd of people who had gathered on the Stone Bridge to see the Emperor on his way to the Old Town. When he saw the imperial carriage approaching, he placed himself with arms outstretched against the carriage. The spectators pelted the Rabbi with stones and excrements, yet he remained motionless, and then he saw that the stones and excrements were changing in the air into roses and violets.

The carriage stopped and the Emperor looked out of the window to see what was going on. The audacious Rabbi came closer, made a low respectful bow, handed the monarch his plea in writing and asked for an audience. The Emperor glanced at the list and ordered the petitioner not to leave his house in the following seven days.

---

[26] Rudolph II (born 1552, died 1612): legendary Bohemian King and Roman-German Emperor from 1576

On the seventh day, a magnificent carriage appeared in front of the little house of Rabbi Loew, who was to be taken to the Emperor.

Rabbi Loew sat with the Emperor and with other scholars and noble men for a long time and they discussed the issues concerning the threatening expulsion. Rabbi Loew asked for mercy of the law and for protection of the Jews in Prague.

On that very day Rudolph II arranged that no inconveniences should happen any more, that every offence must be solved by a just court and that the whole community shall never be held responsible for the guilt of an individual in future.

Many stories are told about the wisdom and competence of Rabbi Loew. His prestige increased day by day and before long it was said in Prague that he was as wise as Solomon[27] himself.

The favour of the Emperor did not last long, however, he was mostly occupied with alchemy and astrology and he left the affairs of the state to his advisers. But they did not want the Jews in Prague and they used every opportunity to incite the Emperor against them. Finally the Emperor tired of all the unending quarrels and pressure from the ghetto, decided that all Israelites should be expelled from the country without delay.

The night after this decree was issued the Emperor had a very strange dream.

He saw himself in a carriage. The area was bare and shadowless and the Emperor was sweating, could hardly breathe because of his thirst. Then he saw a river, he ordered the coachman to stop, got out of the carriage, undressed and stepped into the water to refresh himself. But when he returned to the riverbank he saw that his clothes, his carriage and his entire retinue had vanished.

The Emperor waited sadly for the onset of darkness to reach his castle. Under the protection of the darkness he walked the whole night and by the daybreak he saw Prague already in the distance. He met a group of woodcutters but they insulted him and put the miserable Emperor to flight.

An old beggar gave him a few poor pieces of clothing so that he could go on his way. But then the Emperor saw a fine carriage and he asked the man travelling inside the coach for help. The Emperor was abruptly rejected and told that the Emperor was in his palace and that he had just spoken to him.

It was suddenly clear to the Emperor what was going on. A swindler from his retinue had taken his clothes and his place and pretended to be the Emperor himself.

The Emperor brooded vainly about what to do. He wandered the whole day around the town and became more and more miserable. He was now also convinced that he lost his power as

---

[27] Solomon (born about 965 BC, died 926 BC): King of the empire of the territory of Israel and Judea, an ideal of a wise and powerful ruler

well. Who would now believe him that there is a false Emperor sitting there in the castle and that he himself was not a swindler?

With sore feet and an empty stomach he came to the ghetto. He stopped in front of the Old-New-Synagogue and thought of Rabbi Loew. With the last show of strength he reached his house and was received with the greatest reverence by the Rabbi. After he had washed himself, put on some clothes, ate a little and rested a while, he asked the Rabbi for advice and help.

The Rabbi nodded his head and said: "Every criminal comes back to the place where he committed his crime. Today it will be again very hot and the Emperor's double will undoubtedly go bathing. Where else would he be attracted more to than to the riverbank, where he became Emperor illegally. As he steps into the water, just do the same thing to him that he has done to you!"

The Emperor feeling a new hope promised the Rabbi all the treasure of the world.

But the Rabbi only said sadly: "If you want to give me something, do rather something else instead. Now you know the bitter taste of injustice. What you suffered in filth and dust of the roads, the same awaits our whole nation. Not only for a few hours but for the whole of our life. Therefore I ask you to allow my nation to remain there where we feel at home."

With great pleasure the Emperor issued a new decree in which he annulled his resolution concerning the expulsion. Then he went to the River Vltava to await his double.

He had not long to wait. At the hour that the Rabbi announced, an imperial carriage with the retinue appeared. The swindler got out of the carriage, undressed and jumped in the water. At that moment, the Emperor stepped out from behind the hedge and ordered the coachman to go back to the castle as quickly as possible.

The horses ran as if possessed, the carriage was shaking from side to side over the rough road and then suddenly the Emperor woke up. He was lying in his own bed and then he realised that it was all only a dream. He got up, went to the window and stood there for a long time deep in thoughts. When he returned to his bed, he glanced at his table – and stooped over it as if he had seen a mirage. On the table there were the rags from the beggar who had appeared in his dream and next to them a document compiled and signed by the Emperor.

He was sitting with his head lowered and contemplating for a long time. Early in the morning he passed the document with the decision about the annulment of the expulsion, to his ministers. So Rabbi Loew was able to protect his loyal Jewish community from the hardship of expulsion.

Old post office building in the Jewish Town

The Wine Merchant and His Coachman

The famous Prague Rabbi Jecheskel Landau was sitting in his armchair in his study one day. He was frowning. In front of him on a long table there were countless folio volumes. He was suddenly distracted by a loud creak as if someone had violently ripped open the door and two men entered. The Rabbi recognised his countrymen (he came from Poland) by their traditional costumes. He greeted them and welcomed them with "Scholem alejchem" according to their custom. After the usual questions: Which country are you coming from? Where are you going to? What was your journey like? the Rabbi asked what was their wish. They both began to speak together and Rabbi Jecheskel had to ask one of them to be quiet while the other one spoke. Then, the first man started to tell his story:

"My name is Josef Kohen and I am the son of Simon Kohen, a wine merchant from Warsaw. This man's name is Chajim Geilis and I employed him as my coachman for five years. In that time he has accompanied me on my business trips and he has behaved candidly and honestly. However, on this Rosch-Chodesch[28] day, when I got up that morning (we had just arrived in Austria) and I was looking for my money sack and I soon found that it had disappeared! All my savings, a thousand ducats! So I called Chajim who is standing here as well and asked him if he knew where my money is. He replied scornfully: "Where did you get so much money from in the first place, you are still my coachman, aren't you?

Did you rob someone?" At first I thought Chajim was joking (which he never did before) and I told him to stop pretending. But I soon noticed that this absurd assertion had settled firmly in his head. He claimed with such certainty exactly the opposite of the truth. That I am his coachman and he is my employer. We have agreed to come and ask you, dignified Rabbi, whose wisdom is well known from one end of the world to the other, to determine who is the guilty one. But I, as the deceived, would preferably like to ask you to help me get my thousand ducats back because I have a wife and child at home and the lost sum of money is my entire living. The loss would make me and my whole family

---

[28] Beginning of a month, the first day of the month

beggars." Josef Kohen kept on talking in this tone. When he finally finished, the Rabbi thought it over carefully and then asked Chajim to tell the story from his point of view. Chajim told the same story but with even greater emphasis and sympathy – provoking expressions that he, Chajim, was the deceived one, and Josef Kohen the deceiver.

When they had both finished their stories, the wise Rabbi browsed through the folio volumes for a few minutes. As if it were written there who the wine merchant is and who the coachman. Suddenly he shut the books and spoke strongly to their conscience. But the hidden villain did not confess. Rabbi Jecheskel was a clever man though. He thought of another way how to loosen the tongue of the cunning deceiver. He asked both men to come over at an appointed hour the following day. At the same time he ordered his servant not to let anyone enter his study unannounced.

The next day both Jews from Poland appeared at the Rabbi's house. As

Ritual chalice
from the time
of Rudolph II

40

the servant went to announce them to the Rabbi, they were waiting in the hall. The servant returned soon with a message for them to wait in the anteroom for a while because Rabbi Jacheskel Landau could not receive them yet. When they were talking to each other, the Rabbi rumbled about in his study, then all of a sudden he ripped the entrance door open quite unexpectedly and shouted in a harsh voice: "The coachman is expected!" It was nobody else but Chajim who was quite unprepared for this trick because he was usually called by this name. So he stood up and entered the room. There he was received with a thundering dressing down concerning the punishment. Chajim confessed right away and promised not to lie anymore. Then he returned the stolen thousand ducats remorsefully.

The rumour about this successful trick spread quickly throughout the entire Jewish community. There were crowds in the streets to see the two Jews from Poland who had become famous because of their ignorance. This incident though had the greatest influence on the Chief Rabbi's opponents, who, after Rabbi Landau proved his wisdom and reasonable caution, capitulated and became his best friends.

Not only Prague but the whole of Bohemia was rejoicing when the rumour about this wise method reached the public, which even added to its value. Wherever there was a small gathering of Jews at that time, nobody and nothing else but Rabbi Chaskele Jampolis (he was known by this name because he was often called so in his homeland) and his incident with the two Polish Jews were remembered. Little and unsightly might this event itself have been, but the greater was the Rabbi's reputation and his superior wisdom honoured forever. He proved this only much later in many cases, during the forty years he was in office in Prague. Long after that old people from Prague who personally knew the Chief Rabbi could often be heard saying: "The Zadik was a Nizuz of Schlomo hamelech."[29]

Ever since then Rabbi Jecheskel Landau lived in unquestionable peace in his community and later when his pieces of work were issued, for example Nodabijhuda, Zlach, he had become very famous far and wide among the Talmudic scholars.

---

[29] "The devotee is a spark of Solomon's wisdom."

A street in the Prague Jewish ghetto

Beleles Street

A plague suddenly broke out among the Prague Jews at the time of Emperor Rudolph II. Its victims, however, were mostly children and the adults were usually spared. The Angel of Death raged terribly in the homes of people of Israel. Hundreds of dead bodies were taken to the Bethchajim[30] every day, even every hour. The corpses had to lie there for days before it was possible to bury them. There were not enough hands to dig the graves for the poor little children who had been taken away before their time. And the poisonous fumes from the unburied bodies served only to increase the plague.

The community was beset with misery and lamentations. As the Black Death had developed in the Jewish Town only, it soon became clear that the whole community was being punished for an unknown crime committed by the Jews. Special prayers were said and days of fasting were ordered to expiate for the sins and to beg Heaven for the diversion of the plague. The gravediggers were still continually busy. All the Rabbis and learned men from Prague met then to discuss how to stop the raging of the Angel of Death.

At first the Rabbis tried to find out what caused the plague. It must have been a crime for which such a serious punishment was brought upon the entire community. Yet nobody was able to give a really genuine reason for it.

The Chief Rabbi Loew who had taken post in the discussions, thought long and deeply in his bed the night after the first fruitless discussions. He eventually fell asleep and then had a vivid dream. It was midnight and the prophet Elijah[31] came to him and led him to the Bethchajim where the bodies of the children rose up from their graves. The Rabbi awoke, and for a long time pondered about his dream. It seemed to him that it was God's inspiration on how to get to the root of the real cause of the plague. So he called one of his most courageous disciples and told him: "God, our Lord, sent misery and misfortune to us because we had sinned heavily. In order to find out of which crime are we guilty, muster your courage and go to

---

[30] Bethchajim: the house of life – the Old Jewish Cemetery in Prague
[31] Elijah: "My God is Jahve"; an Israelite prophet who revealed Jahve's claim to exclusivity approximately 850 BC

the Bethchajim around midnight tonight. When you see the dead children rising from their graves in white shrouds, rip one Tachrichim[32] off and bring it to me."

The disciple did what he was told. He went to the cemetery around midnight and, filled with anxious expectation, he waited to see what would happen. He could have been waiting just half an hour when he heard twelve strokes from the Jewish Town Hall. And immediately, there was life under the tombstones. Small children in white shrouds emerged and floating above the graves they began a bizarre ghostly dance. A fit of shivering seized the disciple and all his limbs trembled as he saw the weird performance. But the well being of the Jewish community depended on his courage and so he ripped off the shroud from one of the children and hurried away.

Quite out of breath he arrived at the house of the Rabbi Loew. He told him what he had seen and gave him the shroud of the dead child. Soon after that the Rabbi saw the ghost of a naked child floating nearby. The children carried on dancing in the cemetery. At one hour after midnight all of them scurried back to their graves again. The one child first noticed it was naked and then that its shroud was missing. But that child was not allowed to enter the tomb. It ran quickly to the Rabbi's house and stopped in front of the window. It stretched out its hands and cried, begging and weeping: "Rabbi, give me my Tachrichim!" But the Rabbi held the shroud tightly and said: "If you want your Tachrichim, then first of all you must tell me what was the real cause of this plague."

At first the ghost of the child said nothing but continued to cry over the lost shroud. The Rabbi remained resolute and in the end the little ghost revealed the reason for the plague. Two spouses living in one street not far from the house of Rabbi Loew indulged in an immoral exchange with their wives. That is why the whole community has been punished by the Black Death. It will not end until the two couples are punished. "And now, I have told you the reason for the plague, give me back my Tachrichim!" said the ghost. The Rabbi returned the little shroud and then the ghost went off happily with the Tachrichim to the Bethchajim to rest in its grave again and to enjoy eternal sleep. The two couples that had brought such a great misfortune and misery on the community were strictly punished and the plague was over.

The street where the two couples had lived began to be called by the people Beleles Street – one the women who had committed the sexual offence was called Bella, and the other one was called Ella.

---

[32] Tachrichim: the shroud

The Creation of Golem

It was the year 1580. A priest called Thaddeus – a fanatical anti-Semite – tried again to disrupt the peace and harmony and to bring about discord and disharmony and to evoke new superstitious accusations of blood rituals.

Rabbi Loew soon learned about it and raised a question 'upwards' in his dream to find a solution to the problem how he should fight against the evil enemy.

He received the following alphabetically arranged answer in reply:

"Ata Bra Golem Dewuk Hachomer W'tigzar Zedim Chewel Torfe Jisrael."

"You shall create Golem from clay and may the malicious anti-Semitic mob be destroyed."

Rabbi Loew interpreted the line of strange words so that he should create a living body from clay with the aid of the letters provided from heaven.

He called for Jizchak ben Simson, his son-in-law, and for a disciple of his Jacob ben Chajim Sasson, the Levite[33], and entrusted them with the mystery on how a Golem should be created. "Therefore I ask for your co-operation because for the creation of a Golem, four different elements are required. Jizchak, you are the element of fire; Jacob, you are the element of water and I myself am the element of air. Together we shall create Golem from the fourth element which is the earth."

Then he informed them in detail how they must go through a deep repentance and purify themselves in order to be ready for the grand creation of Golem.

On a fixed day the three men went to the Mikveh (the ritual bath) after midnight. This time they were bathing with special devotion and then they went home without a word. At home they performed Chazot, the midnight lament for Jerusalem, prayed and chanted the relevant psalms. Finally they went to the bank of the River Vltava. There they looked for a place with clay and then set to work immediately.

Chanting the psalms by torchlight they began work in feverish haste. They kneaded and shaped a human figure with all its limbs, from clay, measuring three ells in length. And there was

---

[33] An Israelite tribe (Old Testament) named after Levi, the son of Jacob and Leah

Golem lying in front of them with his face pointing towards the heavens.

The three men then stood at his feet so that they could see his whole face.

He lay there as a dead body, motionless.

Now Rabbi Loew ordered Jizchak, the priest, to walk seven times round the clay mass starting from the right side. He also entrusted him with the Zirufim, those strange words, that he should be saying when walking.

By the time this was finished, the clay mass had become so heated that it radiated like glowing red-hot metal.

Rabbi Loew asked Jacob, the Levite, to walk round Golem in the same manner but this time in reverse beginning from the left side. A specific Zirufim for his element was indicated to him. When the second assistant finished his task steam forced its way out of the trunk of the figure, the body became moist, hair began to appear on its head and also the nails began to grow on its fingers.

Then Rabbi Loew himself walked around Golem and inserted a Schem[34] written on parchment in Golem's mouth. Rabbi Loew bowed towards the east, the west, the south and the north. Then all three of them said in unison the following words: "And the Lord formed the man from the dust of the ground and breathed into his nostrils the breath of life, and the man became a living being."

The three elements – fire, water and air – caused the fourth element, the earth, to become alive. Golem opened his eyes and looked around in amazement.

And Rabbi Loew said to him: "Get on your feet!" and Golem stood up.

Then they dressed him in the garments of a synagogal servant and he soon looked like a common man. Although he could not speak, later this turned out to be an advantage.

At daybreak the four men went home.

On the way, Rabbi Loew said to Golem: "We have created you from a lump of clay. Your mission is to protect the Jews from persecutions. Your name will be Josef and you will live in the Rabbi's house. Josef, you must obey my commands no matter when and where I might send you – to the fire, to the water, to jump from a roof or even to the seabed."

Josef nodded his head and made movements to show his approval.

At home Rabbi Loew said that he had met a dumb stranger on the street and that he felt compassion for him, so had taken him to the Rabbi's house as a servant.

But he prohibited the people in the house to use Golem for private purposes.

---

[34] Schem: from 'Schema' – name. The name of God is to be understood here.

The Torah Scroll that Fell

It happened on the Day of Atonement in 1587 in the Old-New Synagogue when Rabbi Loew was at prayers. The Torah scroll[35] fell down when a member of the community was about to bring it into the Holy Ark[36] after the afternoon lecture. The incident caused consternation among the members of the community assembled there because this was always considered to be a bad omen. Also Rabbi Loew was upset and immediately ordered that all persons present should fast the following day. On Monday night he raised a question in his dream what sins would have caused such a distressing incident. He did not get a clear reply but received an answer consisting of written characters that he did not know how to interpret. So he wrote the characters on a piece of paper and gave it to Golem with instructions to find out the answer.

When Golem saw the piece of paper, he immediately took the book of prayers from a bookcase, he opened it and pointed to every section where the Torah is read on the Day of Atonement in the afternoon. The letters that were shown to Rabbi Loew were the abbreviation of the verse: "Do not have sexual relations with your neighbour's wife and defile yourself with her."

Rabbi Loew knew then that the man who let the Torah fall down, was having an adulterous relationship and that is why the Torah scroll slipped from his hands. He invited the man to his house and he told him privately about the reply that he had received in his dream. Then the weeping man confessed his sins and asked the Rabbi to grant him absolution.

However, Rabbi Loew went even farther – he arranged the divorce of the adulterous wife from her husband in accordance with the Law of Moses.

---

[35] Torah: originally 'Teaching' – the Bible; later the entire book of the Jewish religious teaching
[36] Holy Ark

Rabbi Loew and Golem

Golem Is Enraged

Rabbi Loew established the custom of giving a sort of daily plan to Golem every Friday afternoon because he did not want to be disturbed by him on the Sabbath unless for extremely urgent reasons. Normally, Rabbi Loew would order him not to do anything else on the Sabbath but be on guard.

Once Rabbi Loew forgot to give his daily plan to Golem on Friday afternoon. And so Golem had nothing to do.

It was almost evening and the people were preparing themselves for the reception of the Sabbath. Without any warning Golem was found rampaging around the Jewish Town like a madman, he wanted to demolish everything that got in his way. His inactivity had made him both bored and angry. When the people saw him, they fled shouting: "Josef Golem has gone crazy!"

There was a terrible panic and the news soon reached the Old-New Synagogue where Rabbi Loew was at prayer. He ran out and without seeing Golem he yelled: "Josef, stop it!"

Then the people saw how Golem stopped, motionless, right on the spot where he was. That moment he looked like a pillar and all of his ferocity had vanished.

Rabbi was then told where Golem was standing, he went there and whispered in his ear: "Go home and lay down in the bed!" And Golem followed him as willingly as a child.

Then Rabbi Loew went to the synagogue again and told the congregation to sing one of the Sabbath songs once more. Since that Friday it never happened again that he would forget to give his daily plan to Golem because he knew that Golem would have been capable of devastating the whole of Prague, had he not quietened him in time.

Old Jewish 'Bethchajim' Cemetery in Prague

Golem's End

A long time passed and the community was no longer bothered by any malicious accusations. Rabbi Loew invited his son-in-law Jizchak, the Levite, and his disciple Jacob. Both had participated in the creation of Golem, and he told them: "Golem had outlived his purpose as there are no accusations of blood rituals to fear any more. Therefore we shall take him away from this world."

It was the beginning of the year 1593. Rabbi Loew ordered Golem not to spend that night in the Rabbi's house but to take his bed to the loft of the Old-New Synagogue and to spend the night there. This went on secretly since it was about midnight.

Two hours after midnight, Rabbi Loew's son-in-law and Jacob, the Levite, came to the house of Rabbi Loew. The question whether such a dead man like Golem and like other dead bodies could be regarded as something contagious was raised. This was a very important question because otherwise the priest would not be allowed to assist at the Golem's destruction. However, Rabbi Loew decided that this is out of the question. The three men accompanied by a servant climbed up to the loft where Golem was sleeping.

They began the destruction process. On principle they did everything they had done when creating Golem only in reverse. Had they placed themselves at Golem's feet looking into Golem's face during the process of creation, now they would stand at his head. Also the words from the Genesis were read backwards. After doing this Golem was transformed again into a mass of clay as he was originally. Then Rabbi Loew called the servant, took the candles and told him to undress Golem except for his shirt. He should also burn the clothes without being seen. The stiff Golem was then covered with old prayer shawls and with the rest of the books that were kept in the loft of the synagogue according to Jewish custom.

In the morning it was announced in

the streets of the Jewish ghetto that Josef Golem had escaped from the town during the night. Only few people knew the truth. Rabbi Loew proclaimed in all synagogues and in all houses of prayer that it was strictly prohibited to enter the loft of the Old-New-Synagogue. Also the rest of the books and the hallowed objects were not to be saved there ever again.

A tombstone in the Old Jewish Cemetery

Rabbi Loew and the Rose

The following legend reveals how the Chief Rabbi Loew saved his life once thanks to his own wisdom.

The Prague Jewish community was suffering from the Black Death again. This time it left no one untouched, affecting young and old people alike. There were neither enough gravediggers for digging the graves nor enough space for the graves. Rabbi Loew was almost hundred years old at that time, and his hair and beard were white as snow. He searched in vain in his books of learning for the cause of all this misery, and what should be done to abolish it. Under the greatest stress he remembered his dream from the time of the atrocious children's plague. Accompanied by his Bocherim and the synagogal servants he went to the rear wicket gate of the cemetery at night.

When he was about to take the key, the door opened and a tall, pale, thin man stepped out. He held a tremendously long list of paper in his hand. The wise Rabbi immediately recognised the man who was standing before him – it was Death. Rabbi Loew snatched the list from his bony hand. On it were the names of those who were to die the next day including that of Rabbi Loew and the names of some of his companions were also there. The Rabbi was frightened and tore the list into small pieces.

"You have escaped this time," said Death, "but take care to keep away from me a second time!"

Rabbi Loew thus took heed of this warning. For he knew that Death would be waiting at every corner to outwit him. He took up his books again. And as he was also knowledgeable in mechanics, he created a small device to protect him and always carried it with him. If Death appeared somewhere nearby, the device began to tinkle softly as would an old clock and the Rabbi could escape him.

Death was hiding in a variety of shapes to catch the Rabbi but the wise

Talmudic scholar noticed it every time. The scythe-man once took on the appearance of a huckesteress[37], next time he came as a fisherman offering fish for the Sabbath, then as an old beggar, as a Bocher or as an elegant gentleman to whom he wanted to show his courtesy. But the Rabbi's protective device always warned him in time against any mortal danger.

Many years passed and it was the Rabbi's birthday again. All his disciples, relatives and friends gathered at the Rabbi's house to show him their esteem and gratitude.

The Rabbi was so touched by these expressions of appreciation that he forgot his device in his study. He walked towards his guests with a friendly smile. His youngest granddaughter came as the last one and she gave him a beautiful rose. The Chief Rabbi accepted this fragrant gift with pleasure and smelled it. This was fatal for at that moment he collapsed because Death had been hiding in the rose.

The magic device was tinkling with an almost silver tone in the adjacent room in vain. It rang for a long time until its components broke down, then it stopped forever. No one noticed that a small dewdrop was on one petal of the rose in which Death had come.

The tombstone of the Chief Rabbi is situated near the west wall of the Old Jewish cemetery. He rests there in a temple-like sarcophagus with his wife. The relief of a two-tail lion marks his tombstone. Thirty-three of his favourite Bocherim are buried in the vicinity of his grave.

A cemetery impression

---

[37] huckesteress: small tradesperson

Portal of the
Jewish Town Hall
in the Prague ghetto

Pinkas Street

A poor Jew lived in Prague more than two hundred years ago. During the day, just to keep body and soul together, he would walk through the streets with a bundle on his shoulder and buy up old clothes. At night, however, he studied law in his poor abode by the light of a dim lamp. Despite his diligence his earnings were far from enough to cover his family's expenses. And he and his wife and children would have starved to death were it not for a kind-hearted nobleman who had given his support to this man. He told his protégé to show him each Friday how much he had earned during the week. When it was not enough to celebrate the Sabbath in keeping with the rules and to the law, the nobleman added the missing part. Pinkas – this was the name of the Jew – was told to inform the nobleman prior to other feasts, also about the necessities required for other feast days and then he received money for them.

Poor Pinkas considered the kind-hearted nobleman to be an angel from God. Also the way in which he thanked his benefactor was different. It was more of a prayer to God than an acknowledgement of the good deed. Each time he was given a present by the nobleman he looked up to heaven and said: "God, you do not abandon your children and you have helped me again!" When the nobleman asked him after the feast days how he had spent the time, he always answered: "Oh, God has helped us!"

This behaviour irked the nobleman. He said to himself: "These people are so ungrateful! I overwhelm the Jew with good deeds to help him celebrate his Sabbath and he always says that God had helped him. We'll see if God helps him if I withdraw my support and deny him the usual presents now, before the approaching Passover[38]." There were few days left before the

---

[38] Passover; "When to Lord goes through the land....will pass over that doorway, and he will not permit the destroyer to enter your houses and strike you down." (Exodus 12:23) A feast to commemorate the exodus of the Israelites from Egyptian bondage.

beginning of the holiday when every faithful Jew must provide himself with food for the following eight days. In the several few years Pinkas had been receiving money for the most essential things from the nobleman. But this year his patron wanted to leave it to God's help and when he was humbly reminded by the Jew of the approaching holiday he said: "My dear Pinkas, you must provide yourself for the Matzoth[39] alone this year. I am in difficulties these days. Money has not come and I've had great expenses. Your God will help you in another way." A shadow of sadness appeared on Pinkas's face when he heard these words from his benefactor. Yet he did not lose his firm trust in the God of his fathers. He said sadly but calmly: "Never mind. God will help us!" and he went away. With a sorrowful heart he came home in the evening. His wife who was waiting impatiently and the children, who were looking forward to the promised clothes in advance, met him with hurried questions. "How much did you get this year?" asked his wife. "I haven't got anything," answered her husband sadly, threw his empty sack in the corner of the room and prepared himself for evening prayer. The disappointed wife was nagging, the children were crying and poor Pinkas was worried. Crestfallen he went back to his little chamber, locked the door behind him and studied law in the light of the

gloomy lamp until midnight undisturbed.

Midnight had not yet passed. The children slept on their paltry straw mattresses and his wife also fell asleep moaning. Only Pinkas was sitting over a large folio volume, stroking his long beard thoughtfully and staring in front of him fixedly trying to interpret a difficult contradictory part of the Talmud. All of a sudden, the small window blew open and its shutters rattled. A hideous body burst into the chamber and fell down at Pinkas' feet. Pinkas jumped up aghast, took the thick book and held it in front him as a shield, while his trembling lips were saying a ban formula against evil ghosts. At that moment the laughter of many voices could be heard. This only confirmed the Jew's conviction that Masikim (evil spirits) had come to torment him. He kept holding the book in front of him remaining in that position until his wife, awakened up by the noise, knocked on the locked door of the chamber. This added courage to her frightened husband. He tentatively glanced over the Talmud and saw a grimace similar to that of a man with limbs stretched out in front of him. This repulsive spook was a dead monkey. Since Pinkas had his own strange views about monkeys, this vision only increased his fear. He considered these animals to be half people that the noblemen cared for so as to make them

[39] Matzoth, Mazzes: unleavened bread for Passover ('bread of affliction'); a symbol commemorating the exodus from Egypt that happened so quickly that the bread could be baked only

moral and blissful. He thought such a tame learned monkey could be a Christian Proselyte[40]. The frightened Jew started to ponder over all the sad events of the last year. "They will come now," he said, "to get rid of me and my brethren from this Earth. They will insist that I struck this one here. You, good Lord in heaven, please, take pity on me, a poor man!" Meanwhile the anxious, frightened wife broke the door open violently and asked what had happened. When her husband told her everything, she cried out: "Yes, it is a trick to ruin us. We have to get the dead animal out of the house at once." "But how, and where to?" asked Pinkas. "Should I wrap it up and throw it into water? I could easily fall into the hands of a catchpole, not only that I am not strong enough to carry the dead body away." After a long discussion about this the matter, Pinkas suddenly cried out in a happier

---

[40] Proselyte (from Greek 'the one who converts'): someone who changes from one party or religion to another one; in Antiquity especially pagans who joined Jewish communities

Signet of a Jewish printer's family in Prague (1603)

voice: "Do you know what we shall do? We shall burn the half man. Go on, light the fire and I shall bring in wood." A good strong fire was made in the stove and then Pinkas and his wife took the monkey's feet to drag it to the kitchen. As they were dragging him, there was the sound of a coin rolling on the floor. They dropped the dead monkey and followed the sound. Pinkas took a lamp, his wife a pine spill and they searched the floor eagerly. How happy they were when they caught sight of a ducat glittering in the corner! They grabbed the dead monkey once more with much greater courage and they tried to drag it farther along. And what a surprise! Gold coins fell from the animal's throat. Pinkas looked upward and called in a tone of devotion: "I was young and I have grown old and I have neither seen a pious man abandoned nor his children looking for bread." He took a big knife and started to dismember the animal. He was looking for the source of the money and he soon found it. The stomach of the animal was full of ducats. Pinkas removed them. When there were none left he cut the God sent animal into small pieces and burnt them in flames of the stove. The gold coins were cleaned and put in a bag. The floor was scoured clean and all signs of blood removed. Before dawn there were no traces of the monkey left, except the coins which were in the bag of the delighted Pinkas.

"What you spend on glorification during the Holy days will be richly rewarded by the Lord!" says the Talmud. Poor Pinkas provided everything his wife desired - clothes for the children, flimsy underwear and richly embroided hoods. Neither were delicacies, relishes and beverages such as the best wine and the finest meat missing. Prosperity and pleasure prevailed in the home where just yesterday there had been the direst need. The Passover has not been celebrated in such a joyful way and with such piety and prayers since the people of Israel were expelled from Egypt, as it was at the Pinkas's this time. An eight-branched chandelier above the table and wall-lights with polished round shades dispersed bright light throughout the clean, warm room. Next to the table was an upholstered couch decorated with large flowers. This was for the host who was stretched out on it at full length wrapped in a shroud. The hostess sat opposite to husband. She was dressed in a long richly folded Spencer and had a bonnet decorated with stiff lace and wide silken ribbons. She was filling the glasses with wine. The children sat around the table happily waiting for the coming events. On the table stood round pewter containing three Matzoth wrapped in a large cloth. Horseradish, cress, baked eggs; a joint of roast meat and a container of salted water were also there. The bowl was raised by the people around the table who said the following verses: "This is the bread of the hardship, which our fathers ate in the land of Mizrajim[41]. He who is hungry come, eat with us." Suddenly there was the sound of a carriage. Before Pinkas finished what he was saying someone knocked on the window.

Pale from fright Pinkas rose from his coach to find out who had disturbed them. He asked with trembling voice who it was at the window. "Open the door, Pinkas! I have come to celebrate the Passover with you today!" a voice replied. At first they thought that the late guest was no one else but the prophet Elijah who visited the pious people at this time. For this reason a special glass for him must be filled on the table. The bar was removed quickly, the door opened and – the nobleman, Pinka's patron, came in. "Do not let me disturb you at your prayers. But – what do I see!" he exclaimed looking round the room in amazement. "Have you become a rich man suddenly?" "Yes," said the Jew laughing. "God the Almighty has helped me. A few days ago I was so very poor and had no idea that I might celebrate this Passover properly, as every Jew is expected to do. However, God helped me and I am a rich man now." "Would you mind telling me," the nobleman said, "how it happened that your situation changed so quickly?" "No," answered Pinkas and related the true story to his patron, who listened attentively. When the Jew mentioned the monkey, the nobleman could no longer conceal his astonishment and exclaimed: "What! A dead monkey? It must have been mine. That would be incredible. My monkey passed away suddenly three days ago. I had it taken from the house because I did not want to see it anymore. Nevertheless, what does this have to do with your good fortune?" When Pinkas heard these words, he went to a box and unlocked it. He took out the large pouch and handed it to the patron saying: "Everything except the few coins that I spent in order to celebrate the Holy day is there." "What do you mean?" asked the nobleman in amazement. "Well, the monkey had the gold inside its stomach. But as the monkey belonged to you, so does the gold," answered the Jew. Then the nobleman turned to his servant who was standing a short distance away. He asked: "Do you happen to know more details about the story?" "Forgive me, my lord," replied the terrified servant, "the house servant wanted to play a prank on the poor Pinkas. He threw the animal into his chamber. Several other servants knew about it." "What! The house servant? The prank turned out surprisingly," said the nobleman smiling. "I had the poor boy put in jail despite his innocence. However, it may have been a penalty for the crime he had committed

---

41 Mizrajim: a Hebrew name for Egypt

Jewish inhabitants of the Prague ghetto

against poor Pinkas. The foolish animal wanted to imitate me and had eaten the gold on my table, which was then missing. The monkey saw that I put the lighter coins between my teeth to mark them and then it thought that they were edible!" "The gold is here," Pinkas interrupted him and passed the pouch over to his patron. "No, my honest Pinkas. The God of your fathers gave you this treasure and it shall be yours. I refused to give you the usual donation this year to see if God would really help you without me. You always kept saying: God has helped me. I understand now that your confidence is Him is justified. I shall spend this evening with you," he said. "So do not let yourself be disturbed and continue as if I were not here. My wife should come soon and learn about this miraculous coincidence." The carriage was sent away. In a short time the wife

of the nobleman arrived and they both stayed on until Pinkas, the Seder[42], ended with the line: "God will kill the Death Angel once!"

Pinkas gained great wealth in few years because of his diligence, wisdom and with the help of the nobleman. His honesty and wisdom increased his reputation among the people. And soon he was elected the Mayor of the Jewish community. Nevertheless, he was always honest and humble just as when he had been poor. His house was a meeting place of the wisest Rabbis. His hand was open to everyone who was in need and the hungry poor people ate at his table every day. He had several dwellings built for the poor in the street where he lived. A magnificent synagogue was erected at his expense, which still today carries his name. And that street is called the Pinkas Street.

---

[42] Seder: a section from the Bible or the Talmud; a name for the evening of the Passover when the Haggadah is read

The legends originate from the following:

Sippurum, Prager Sammlung Jüdischer Legenden in neuer Auswahl und Bearbeitung; Wien und Leipzig 1926.

Bloch, Chajim: Der Prager Golem; Berlin 1920.

Das Panorama des Universums zur erheiternden Belehrung für Jedermann und alle Länder; Prag 1843.

A supplement to **"Ost und West"**; Prag 1843.